ACROSTIC DIARY

GOWRI

I dedicate this piece of writing to my dear ones who constantly encouraged me on my every prose. Their best regards and consistent support has brought till this.

Thank you everyone.

with love and regards,

Gowri...

Contents

Foreword *vii*

Preface *ix*

Acknowledgements *xi*

Prologue *xiii*

1. Grow Patience To Wait 1
2. Make It Happen 2
3. Self Love 3
4. Congratulations 4
5. Miss You 5
6. Kick Off Excuses 6
7. Comparison 7
8. Practice 8
9. Change Is Eternal 9
10. Accept 10
11. Authentic 11
12. Its Okay 12
13. Nature 13
14. Questions 14
15. Secret 15
16. Simple Life 16
17. Exhausted 17
18. Smile 18
19. Interest 20
20. My Wish List 22

Contents

21. This Too Shall Pass 23

Best Regards 25

Foreword

Dear readers,

This is a collection of Acrostics (poem in which the combination of first letter present you a word or phrase), the outcome of a tiny creative that rooted up in my heart and mind whic has been develop over a year. I bagged up the theme of each prose from my day-to-day life which makes you feel sailing on the same boat at the moment you walk through the lines.

Preface

This is the colection of acrostic poems by an 23 rd young poet, who have started to write on her 21 st birthday and publishing on every year from then. The stanzas in the prose symbolizes different circumstances of pros and cons faced over a year. Whatever you go through pen down always makes heart and mind lighter.

Always remember - " This too shall pass through"

Acknowledgements

My sincere gratitude to all readers for stepping into the garden of phrases that defines life of people.

I owe my sincere gratitude to Notion press

Prologue

Always remember,
One day you will reach a place where you actually wanted to be,
Believe in you ,
Wait for the time,
Be consistent on your efforts,
May be your Runway is long,
Because huge take off needs long runways....

1. Grow Patience to Wait

Go by the flow with self compassion
Row your boat with trust and passion;
Obtain enough optimistic way
Windfall may hug you today;

Preseverence is the rope
Anticipation is the scope;
Timely act builds path that lasts ever
Initiate again despite of fear;
Embolden yourself day by day
Nothing is permanent to be so grey;
Change is the only eternal one
Exuberance make things done;

Today teach us something new
Owe thanks to lessons you pursue;

Watch your way not others play
Accomplishment may be long away;
It's time to at least walk or crawl
Think big even you implement small.

-SGD

#Acrostic

2. Make It Happen

3. Self Love

Seek the happiness in and melt
Emphasize yourself the hilt
Lean yourself for not to break out
Face but not dive in predicament

Live in present, black past - buried
Ocean of dark thoughts - deleted
Values of endeavours - cultivated
Everyday /one is unique - denoted
#acrostic
-SGD

4. Congratulations

5. Miss You

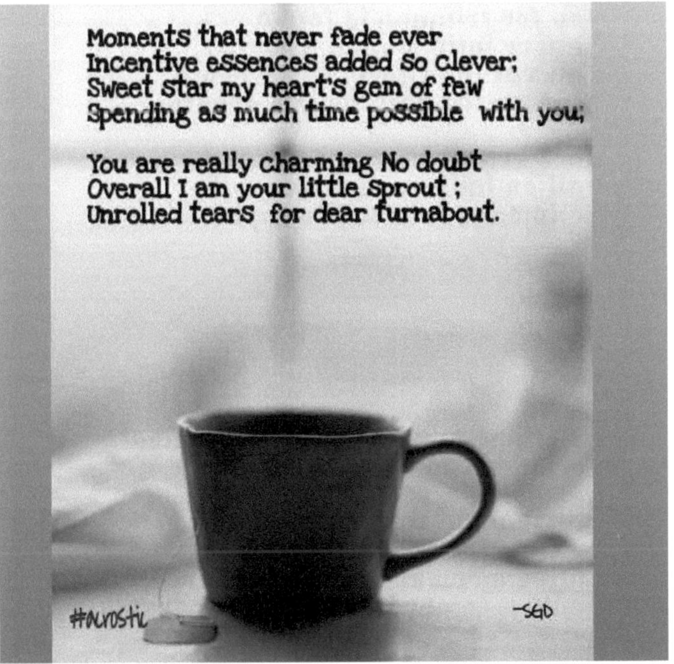
Moments that never fade ever
Incentive essences added so clever;
Sweet star my heart's gem of few
Spending as much time possible with you;
You are really charming No doubt
Overall I am your little sprout ;
Unrolled tears for dear turnabout.
#acrostic
-SGD

6. Kick Off Excuses

Key for triumph is found
Ignore intimidation at daunt,
Conceal the efforts underneath
Keep on the path to new sheath.

Once begun dare not to finish
Fall on failures don't vanish,
Follow up yourself to replenish;

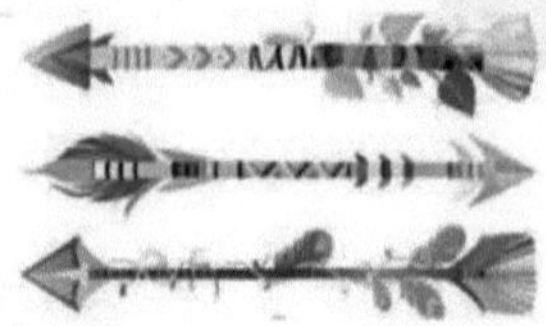

Exist and survive to become fittest
Xeric shift to spring is nearest,
Compete and crush haste & wastes
Utilize your clock solely in tots;
Swedge for dream in silence
Enlive moments with fair glance,
Smile wholehearted at perseverance.

#acrostic

-SGD

7. Comparison

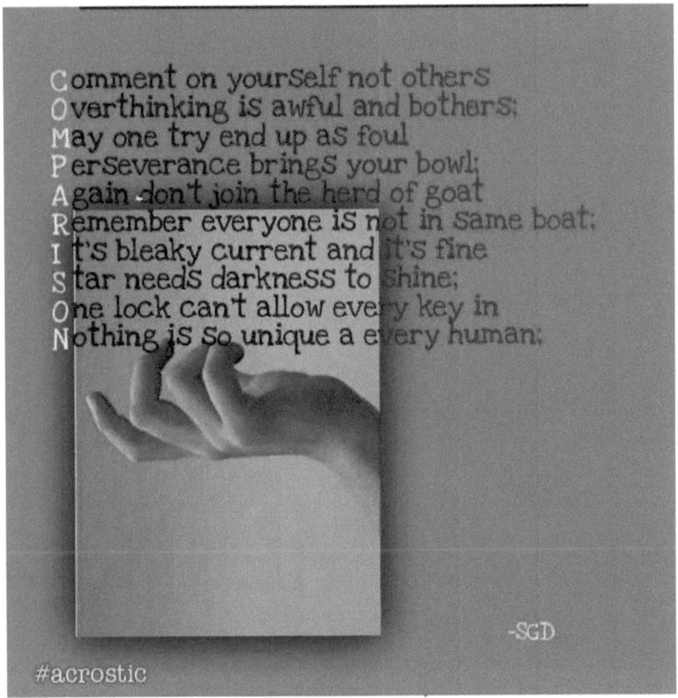

8. Practice

#acrostic
repare yourself for a change
eassign the task with courage
lign your scheme of life
hange prevails after strife
ime replies uncertainities
gnition may he small in size
onsistency in action is notion
very day is nature's potion.
-SGD

9. Change is Eternal

10. Accept

#acrostic
Activities should be strived towards height
Comparison with dead past is solely waste
Contributions towards growth absolutely must
Emotions on missed chance to be erased
Push away as far as the lowliness in you
Timely apt thoughts may raise in you.
-SGD

11. Authentic

12. Its Okay

In any day of life's hind
Took amiss or flaw found
Slavishly scratching the mind

Overthinking kills apt thought
Kindly warm the little heart
Accept it wholly at first
Yes, not carried in next

- SGD

#ACROSTIC

13. Nature

Nourishes mind with optimistic thought
Assist you to retain the warm heart - As
Tender as the care shown by loved one
Uniquely speaks to the soul in everyone
Repair each and everything of course
Equality is its only law in force.
-SGD

14. Questions

15. Secret

#acrostic
Some strengths that stays in you strongly
Eagerly anticipated by the world frequently
Conquest yourself to compile own future gist
Retaining scant of it is requisite to exist
Everything in air is will never give peace to your soul
Testing your endurance on our steps towards goal
-SGD

16. Simple Life

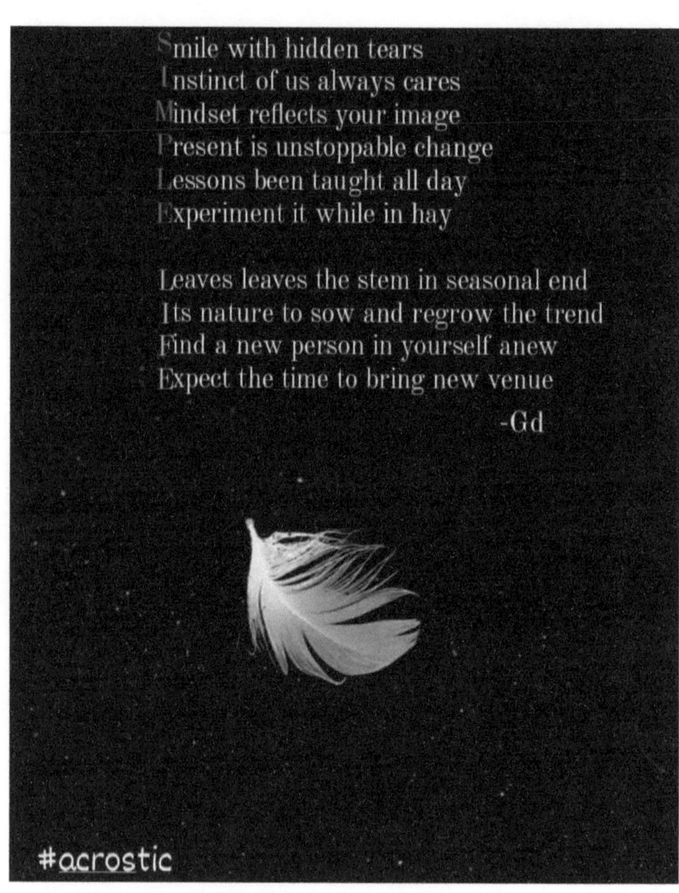

17. Exhausted

18. Smile

SIMPLE TO MAKE ANYWAYS
MOST TOUGH TO ADAPT ALWAYS
IDEAL WAY TO MOVE ON PACE
LOVELY WAY TO FORGET BAD DAYS
ELEGANT MODE TO LOOK WITH GRACE
-Gd
#acrostic
STRONG ENOUGH TO THRIVE YOU
MILES IT TRAVEL WITH YOU
IMPLIES AN INFANT IN YOU
LONG ENOUGH TO HOLD YOU
EVER CURVE DOWNWARDS FOR YOU

19. Interest

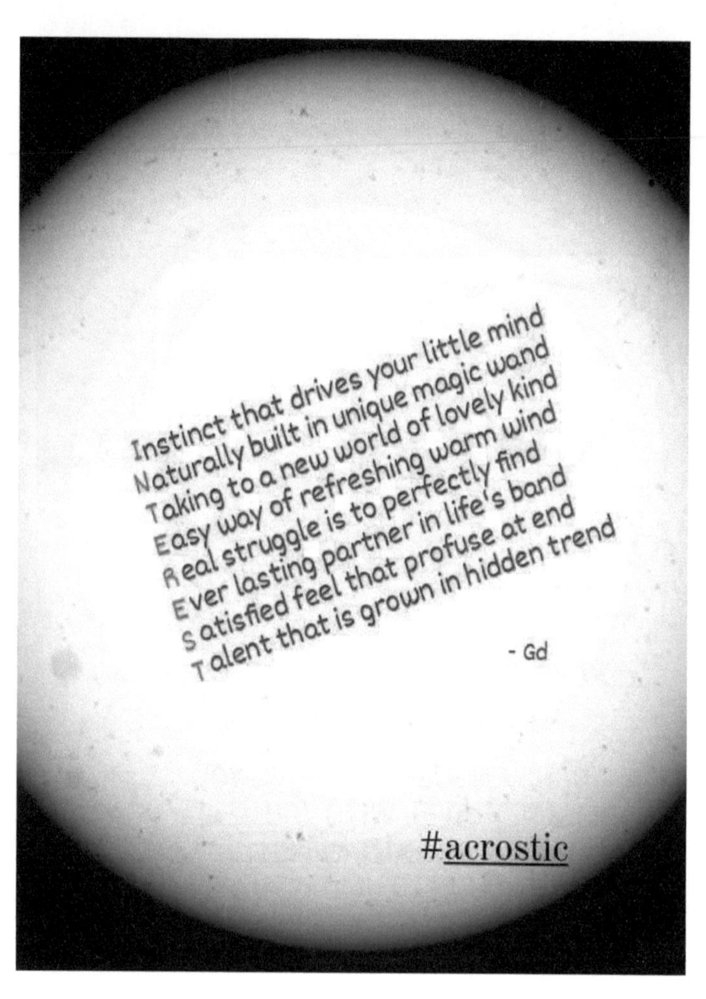

Instinct that drives your little mind
Naturally built in unique magic wand
Taking to a new world of lovely kind
Easy way of refreshing warm wind
Real struggle is to perfectly find
Ever lasting partner in life's band
Satisfied feel that profuse at end
Talent that is grown in hidden trend
- Gd
#acrostic

20. My Wish List

21. This Too Shall Pass

Best Regards

Dear Readers,

I wish you all best of lucks to achieve greater heights in coming up days. I hope that you have enjoyed the essence of the stanzas with the message hidden in them.

Comments and suggestions on this collection of prose are most welcomed at diaryofbuddingpoet@gmail.com.

With love and regards

_Gowri

9 798887 497907

Printed by Libri Plureos GmbH in Hamburg, Germany